CANBERRA

AEROGUIDE 34: ENGLISH ELECTRIC CANBERRA PR Mk 9

ROGER CHESNEAU

Ad Hoc PUBLICATIONS

INTRODUCTION

SUSTAINED, powered flight has been known to mankind for a century or so, and for more than half that period one aircraft has served continuously in the front line, all over the world, in various guises and in a plethora of roles. One is hard-pressed to think of any other aircraft—anywhere—that shares this proud and noble record. The English Electric Canberra has served in front-line RAF squadrons contemporarily with the Spitfire and with the Eurofighter Typhoon; dozens of fighter, attack and reconnaissance aircraft types have come and gone, but the 'Cranberry', as it is affectionately known in some quarters, has remained in service, adapted and upgraded better to fit its role requirements, but fundamentally unchanged in appearance—simply because it has proved to be such an outstanding design. 'Irreplaceable' is perhaps too strong an adjective to apply even to the Canberra, but the aircraft has come closer to deserving such an accolade than almost any other.

The development of the Canberra from its beginnings as a gleam in the eye of its designers is briefly covered in AEROGUIDE 35, which deals with the initial B Mk 2 bomber version of the aircraft and its direct derivatives, and so will not be discussed in the present book; instead, the pages that follow will concentrate on the final photographic-reconnaissance variant, the PR Mk 9, which, as these words are written, is due to be withdrawn from service in a few weeks' time, thus bringing to an end over 55 years of Canberra operations in the Royal Air Force. Brief reference is also made to earlier photographic-reconnaissance variants, the PR.3 and the PR.7.

Even a cursory glance through the pages of this book will make it obvious that the author has been fortunate to have benefited from willing and exceptionally generous assistance by the members of No 39 (1 PRU) Squadron, and in this context he would like particularly to thank the CO, Wing Commander Clive Mitchell, for permission to visit the Squadron on a number of occasions, and Flight Sergeant Simon Roberts, whose ready help has been of immeasurable value and who has cheerily weathered a good deal of pestering from the author. The ground images taken at RAF Marham were acquired by kind permission of the Station CO, Group Captain Greg Bagwell, to whom thanks are also due; some of the photographs were taken at RAF Wyton in the early 1980s, and thanks go also therefore to the officers and airmen who

Below: One of the very last: Canberra PR Mk 9 XH134 comes into land at RAF Marham, its home base, a few months before the type was finally withdrawn from service.
Right: PR Mk 9 XH168 at Wyton in August 1980, at which time Canberras were still painted in grey-green disruptive camouflage.

assisted at that time, principally of No 1 Photographic Reconnaissance Unit (to which the Mk 9s were then assigned) and of the Canberra Servicing Flight and the Electrical Engineering Squadron.

For their generous assistance, and for advice and permissions in other respects, the author and publishers gratefully acknowledge the following: BAe Systems; Del Holyland and the Martin-Baker Aircraft Company; George Canciani; Sergio Gava; Fergal Goodman; Joop de Groot; Michael Hall; Lieuwe Hofstra; Phil Jarrett; Ron Kellenaers; Geoffrey Lee; Ian Powell; Ray Rimell; Álvaro Romero; Simon Thomas; Michael Vaeremans; Dick Ward; and Steve Williams. **R.D.C.**

THE REQUIREMENT

FROM the dawn of aviation, the value of the aircraft as a reconnaissance platform has been very well understood; indeed, many military strategists during the early years of the twentieth century envisaged reconnaissance as the *only* role in which the aircraft could be a valuable asset. The better informed one is about the strengths and weaknesses of the enemy, the more efficiently one can prosecute hostilities. The importance of reconnaissance, and its effect on the enemy, was quickly recognised in the Great War that followed inasmuch as air forces very hastily armed their aircraft, primarily in an effort to deny the enemy the advantage of surveying their dispositions, troop movements, equipment, etc., by shooting down his reconnaissance aeroplanes ('scouts') and thereby preventing them from gathering intelligence or, at least, from bringing it safely back to the home front.

Thus was born in effect the 'hybrid' reconnaissance aircraft—a machine not only tasked with the gathering of information but also having the capacity to defend itself against a marauding enemy. This type of aircraft has been developed over the decades, during which time the emphasis has switched from the arming of reconnaissance aircraft to the equipping of standard combat types with a reconnaissance capability—a capability that is found today on the front-line combat inventory of most of the world's air forces. However, whilst this multi-role function is considered acceptable for short-range tactical missions, long-distance reconnaissance calls for a machine with rather special characteristics.

THE MISSION

Several centuries B.C. the Chinese writer Sun Tsu, in his treatise *The Art of War*, was urging military commanders to 'Know thine enemy as thyself'; and, of course, there is the time-honoured military adage 'Time spent on reconnaissance is never wasted'—as true today as it ever was. In fact, reconnaissance is, arguably, the most valuable military activity: after all, if one does not know the strengths and weaknesses of the enemy, one is unlikely to be able to make effective contact, either directly or indirectly; moreover, military action is governed largely by what the enemy is doing, or is likely to do in the near future.

All military combat aircraft are, in a sense, reconnaissance aircraft, if only because combat pilots need to judge how best to take action once their target, or objective, is encountered. This is why so many combat aircraft have, historically, incorporated in their systems some sort of reconnaissance aid—an observer, a telescopic sight, a camera—to assist the pilot prior to and during in an engagement. However, the Canberra PR series were never combat aircraft, nor were they intended to be: inheriting the tasks of the fast and high-flying wartime Mosquito, their role was to fly speedily and at altitude, evading any would-be pursuers by sheer velocity: it has to be remembered that the aircraft's top speed of some 500 knots, while seemingly pedestrian these days, was very swift when the design was being evolved in the late 1940s.

Their task was strategic, photographing swathes of territory rather than 'point targets' and carrying out area survey rather than what would nowadays be termed tactical reconnaissance. However, owing to the technical quality of the cameras installed, fine detail was routinely

Above: A B.E.2 reconnaissance aeroplane flies over trenches of the Western Front during World War I.
Below: Canberra PR Mk 9 XH134 in the skies above East Anglia in 1993.

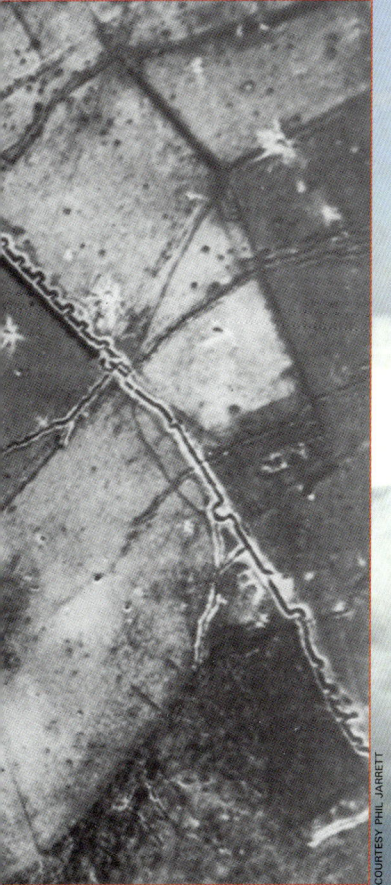

Right, upper: The Supermarine Spitfire PR Mk XI. A PR Spitfire of an earlier mark photographed the German battleship *Bismarck* in a Norwegian fjord in May 1941, enabling the Admiralty to track her movements and bring her to battle.
Right, lower: A De Havilland Mosquito PR Mk 34—the immediate predecessor of the PR Canberras.

available from the images captured, the major problem then arising being the number of man-hours required to interpret the vast acreages of film.

Aspects of the Canberra PR.9's work have always, for obvious reasons, been classified, and this remains the case even to this day. In later years, although the aircraft was an exceptionally useful tool in areas of conflict, it also played a significant part in gathering information for the planners of humanitarian relief by overflying areas of the world smitten by disaster, both natural and man-made, and recording the evidence. Truly have these aircraft, and their flight crews, ground crews, liaison personnel and photographic staff, rendered magnificent service. High-technology satellites and UAVs (Unmanned Air Vehicles) notwithstanding, they will be very sorely missed.

THE EARLY MARKS

ALTHOUGH the Canberra was conceived as an unarmed, high-altitude bomber fulfilling the role hitherto the province of the Mosquito, it very quickly became apparent that, as with its illustrious predecessor, a multitude of other tasks could readily be accommodated with little modification necessary to the airframe. The potential of the aircraft for photographic reconnaissance duties was one of the first of these, and work, to Air Ministry Specification PR.31/46, began in late 1946 even as the detail design of the bomber version was in progress. Extending the fuselage by 14in permitted the installation of a camera bay forward of the bomb bay, which itself was converted to accommodate extra fuel forward and flares for nocturnal photography aft. Further modifications allowed the aircraft to carry still more fuel, raising the total capacity by over 500 gallons and giving the aircraft a range of over 3,000 miles, while a new glazed nose enabled the navigator to sight photographic targets visually.

The first flight of the PR Mk 3 (as the first photo-reconnaissance variant was dubbed) took place on 19 March 1950 from Salmesbury, but owing to problems with vibration and buffeting it took some two and a half years for the aircraft to enter RAF service, the receiving unit being No 541 Squadron (which spent much of its time with the aircraft 'ironing out the wrinkles') at RAF Benson from November 1952, and another two years for the mark to reach an operational front-line unit, No 69 Squadron at RAF Gütersloh in West Germany.

Thirty-five PR.3s were built, and by early 1954, when the last of them were being delivered, their successors, PR Mk 7s, were already arriving for service with Nos 540 and 542 Squadrons at RAF Wyton; indeed, the first batch of Mk 7s started life as Mk 3s but were modified as they were being manufactured. The problem with the PR.3 had been, surprisingly, insufficient range for the sorties deemed necessary over the coming years, and so the integral wing fuel tanks that had been developed for the bomber version of the Canberra and trialled in the B.5 prototype were incorporated into the PR.3 airframe, together with a strengthened undercarriage, anti-skid brakes and uprated Avon Mk 109 (RA.7) instead of Mk 101 (RA.3) jet engines, each of the new powerplants providing an extra 1,000lb of thrust.

The PR.7 equipped almost a dozen RAF squadrons and as a result of a programme of refurbishment was able to perform first-rate service into the 1980s. Over seventy examples were built (including those aircraft that started life as PR.3s), and the type eked out its days at RAF Wyton conducting a variety of tasks for the community of Canberra squadrons based there. Versions of both the PR.3 and PR.7 were supplied to overseas customers, the Indian Air Force buying ten PR.57/67s and the Venezuelan Air Force a couple of PR.83s; in each case these purchases were part of a package also involving Canberra bombers, bomber/intruders and trainers.

The final photographic reconnaissance Canberra variant was the PR.9—the principal subject of this book—which, although it started life as a logical development of the PR.7, in the event turned out rather differently.

Background image: Canberra PR Mk 3 WE146—not a standard service PR.3 but an aircraft allocated to the RAF's Meteorological Flight for weather research.
Below: PR Mk 7 WJ817 in the markings of No 13 Squadron.

Right, top: PR.7 WT520 in early camouflage and showing the fixed canopy characteristic of most Canberra marks. Both the Mk 3 and the Mk 7 had a glazed nose. The camera 'windows' can be seen just aft of the nosewheel.

Right, centre: A PR.7 of No 31 Squadron (upper photograph) and one from No 231 Operational Conversion Unit at Wyton in 1993 (lower photograph). The latter aircraft shows evidence of equipment upgrades and features the Canberra's detachable 244-gallon wing-tip fuel tanks.

Right, bottom: PR.7 WJ817 again, this time at Wyton and in a very sorry state, apparently having been cannibalised and utilised for target practice.

THE EARLY MARKS 7

MARK NINE

FORTY-SIX years of service—not as many as for the *genre* as a whole, and not as many as the T Mk 4 trainer notched up in RAF colours (which totalled well over fifty), but an impressive record nevertheless. That is the length of time the Canberra PR.9 was in the front line, and although threatened with retirement on more than one occasion during that period the aircraft proved to be so valuable an asset that it saw off all opposition; indeed, such was the robustness and reliability of the PR.9 that it was mainly on grounds of cost (the cost of refurbishing the aircraft, particularly to renew the pressurisation system), because of the revolution in photographic technology of recent years (the waning importance of 'wet film', the miniaturisation of cameras) and because of the steadily diminishing stock of spares (for example, for its Avon engines) that the decision finally to withdraw was made.

GENESIS

The service requirement for the Canberra HA (High-Altitude) PR Mk 9 dated back to 1953 and arose from the quest for an ever greater ceiling, exceeding significantly the 50,000ft (or thereabouts) of which the PR.3 and PR.7 were capable. The first aircraft started life as a standard PR Mk 7, equipped with 11,500lb thrust Avon RA.24 engines and with a wing of increased span and inboard area in order to reduce the loading at high altitudes. However, during trials of the aircraft, WH793, it was discovered that the new wing did not perform as hoped: 55,000 feet could be attained with ease, but the 70,000-plus objective proved to be beyond reach—at least, initially.

Left: WH793 was the prototype for the Canberra PR.9 though retained many features of the PR.7. It was converted for trials by D. Napier & Son at Luton, principally to test the revised wing layout.

Main image: XH131 showing her nether regions at Kleine Brogel, Belgium, 20 July 2005. Of note beneath the wing are the Doppler panel and landing light (port side only), the deployed 'finger' type air brakes and the black rectangles of the chaff/flare dispensers.
Right: XH167 at Wyton in May 1979, in 'low-level' (!) tactical camouflage.

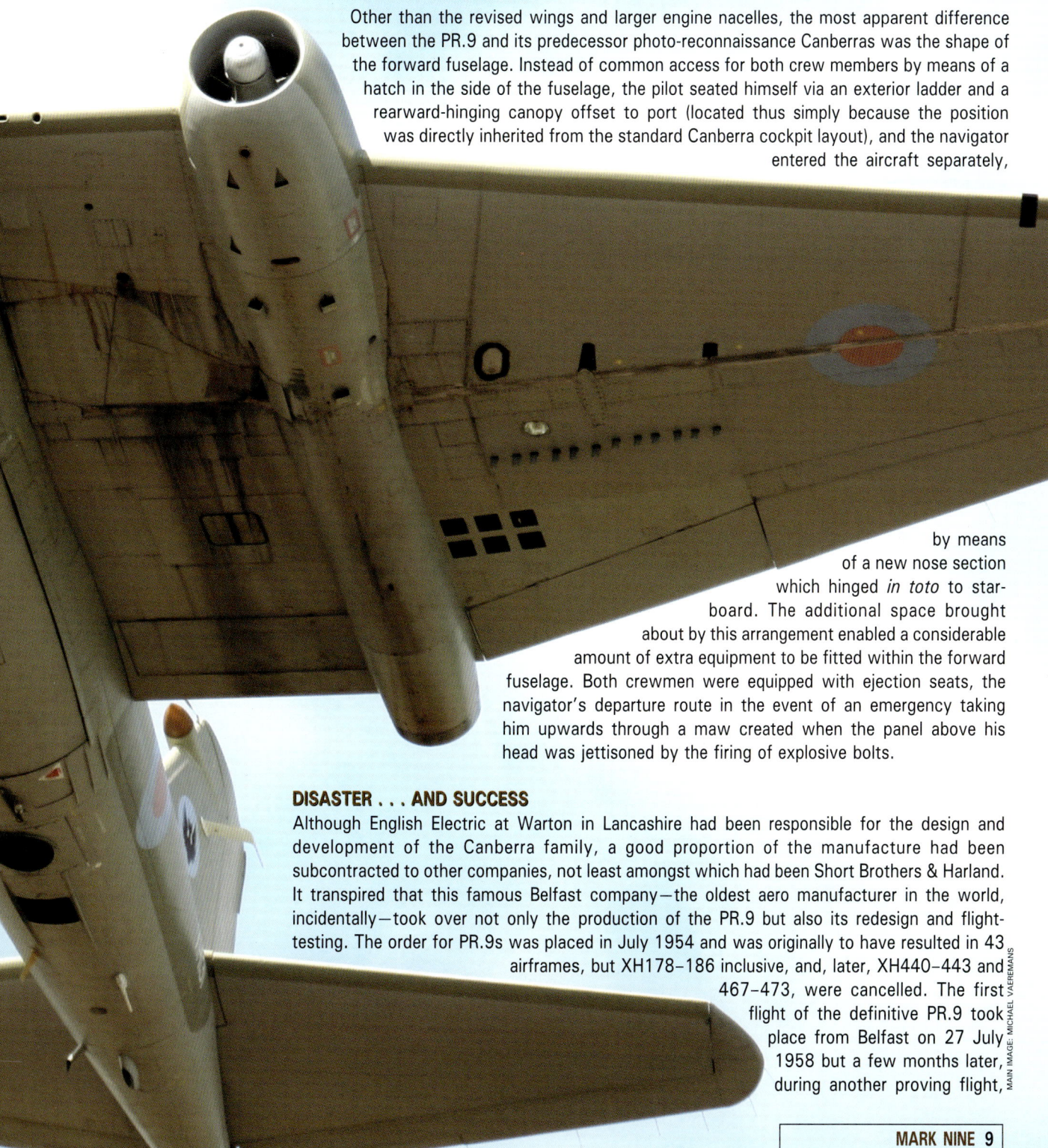

Other than the revised wings and larger engine nacelles, the most apparent difference between the PR.9 and its predecessor photo-reconnaissance Canberras was the shape of the forward fuselage. Instead of common access for both crew members by means of a hatch in the side of the fuselage, the pilot seated himself via an exterior ladder and a rearward-hinging canopy offset to port (located thus simply because the position was directly inherited from the standard Canberra cockpit layout), and the navigator entered the aircraft separately, by means of a new nose section which hinged *in toto* to starboard. The additional space brought about by this arrangement enabled a considerable amount of extra equipment to be fitted within the forward fuselage. Both crewmen were equipped with ejection seats, the navigator's departure route in the event of an emergency taking him upwards through a maw created when the panel above his head was jettisoned by the firing of explosive bolts.

DISASTER . . . AND SUCCESS

Although English Electric at Warton in Lancashire had been responsible for the design and development of the Canberra family, a good proportion of the manufacture had been subcontracted to other companies, not least amongst which had been Short Brothers & Harland. It transpired that this famous Belfast company—the oldest aero manufacturer in the world, incidentally—took over not only the production of the PR.9 but also its redesign and flight-testing. The order for PR.9s was placed in July 1954 and was originally to have resulted in 43 airframes, but XH178–186 inclusive, and, later, XH440–443 and 467–473, were cancelled. The first flight of the definitive PR.9 took place from Belfast on 27 July 1958 but a few months later, during another proving flight,

XH129 caught fire and crashed; the pilot was saved but unfortunately the navigator perished. The fault was shown to lie in the wing-root attachment fairing, but redesigned components in this area were subsequently demonstrated to be satisfactory and the aircraft was eventually accepted into the Royal Air Force in April 1960.

EVOLVING REQUIREMENTS

The PR.9 has been deployed all over the world during the last forty-odd years, quietly going about its invaluable work, sometimes publicised, sometimes not, and not infrequently — in particular early in its career — clandestinely. It quickly achieved fame (retrospectively, as it were), for being the aircraft that photographed Soviet vessels transporting nuclear missiles to the Caribbean in 1962, providing the US President, John F. Kennedy, with the unequivocal

Above: XH137 fresh off the production line, in the sprayed 'aluminium' paint-work that was characteristic of all PR.9s when they first entered service. The beautiful aerodynamic shape of the Canberra is never more evident than when the aircraft is depicted in this finish.

Left: : PR.9 production at Short Brothers & Harland's facility at Queen's Island, Belfast, circa 1958. It will be evident that the aircraft in the foreground does not as yet have the hinged nose unique to the mark, nor for that matter the navigator's ejection hatch.
Right: An early test flight, the original glazed nose of the PR.9 clearly apparent. It is difficult to believe that this is the same aircraft as that depicted across the previous two pages — almost fifty years later.
Below:: Two pristine PR.9s await test flights at Queen's Island, 1959.

10 CANBERRA PR9

SHORTS SC.9

One Canberra Mk 9, XH132, was diverted from the Short Bros. production line and modified for duties as a trials aircraft. It served for many years in this capacity, primarily with the Royal Radar Establishment, under whose auspices it appeared in a variety of different colour schemes (two of which are depicted at right). Amongst its tasks were the development of the De Havilland Red Top infra-red anti-aircraft missile (as carried by RAF Lightning interceptors) and of the BAe Sky Flash medium-range AAM (as carried today by Tornado interceptors).

proof with which he could confront Nikita Krushchev and demand that he halt the deployments. The Cuban Missile Crisis, as it was to become known, came close to embroiling NATO and the Warsaw Pact in thermonuclear war, and it was only when the Soviets backed down that the world could collectively sigh with relief. Throughout the 'Cold War' years of the 1960s–1980s the PR.9 served with unfailing distinction over troublespots as and when surveillance—both overland and maritime—was called for. In recent times, albeit with the number of aircraft in

ENGLISH ELECTRIC CANBERRA HA PR Mk 9 SPECIFICATIONS AND PRODUCTION DATA

Engines	Two Rolls-Royce RA.24 Avon Mk 206 turbojets each rated at 11,250lb (5,100kg)
Dimensions	
Length	66ft 8in (20.32m) overall; later 66ft 6½in (20.28m) overall
Wingspan	67ft 10½in (20.69m); later 67ft 11½in (20.71m)
Height	15ft 7in (4.75m)
Wing area	1,045 sq ft (97.1m^2)
Take-off weight (max.)	57,500lb (26,100kg)
Performance	
Max. speed	560mph (490kts; 900kph) 'at altitude'
Max. operating altitude	70,000ft (21,300m) approx. (designed)
Range	4,000 miles (6,400km) approx.
Production:	Twenty-two aircraft (XH129–131, XH133–137, XH164–177) plus one SC.9 (XH132)

CANBERRA PR.9 CAMERA SUITE

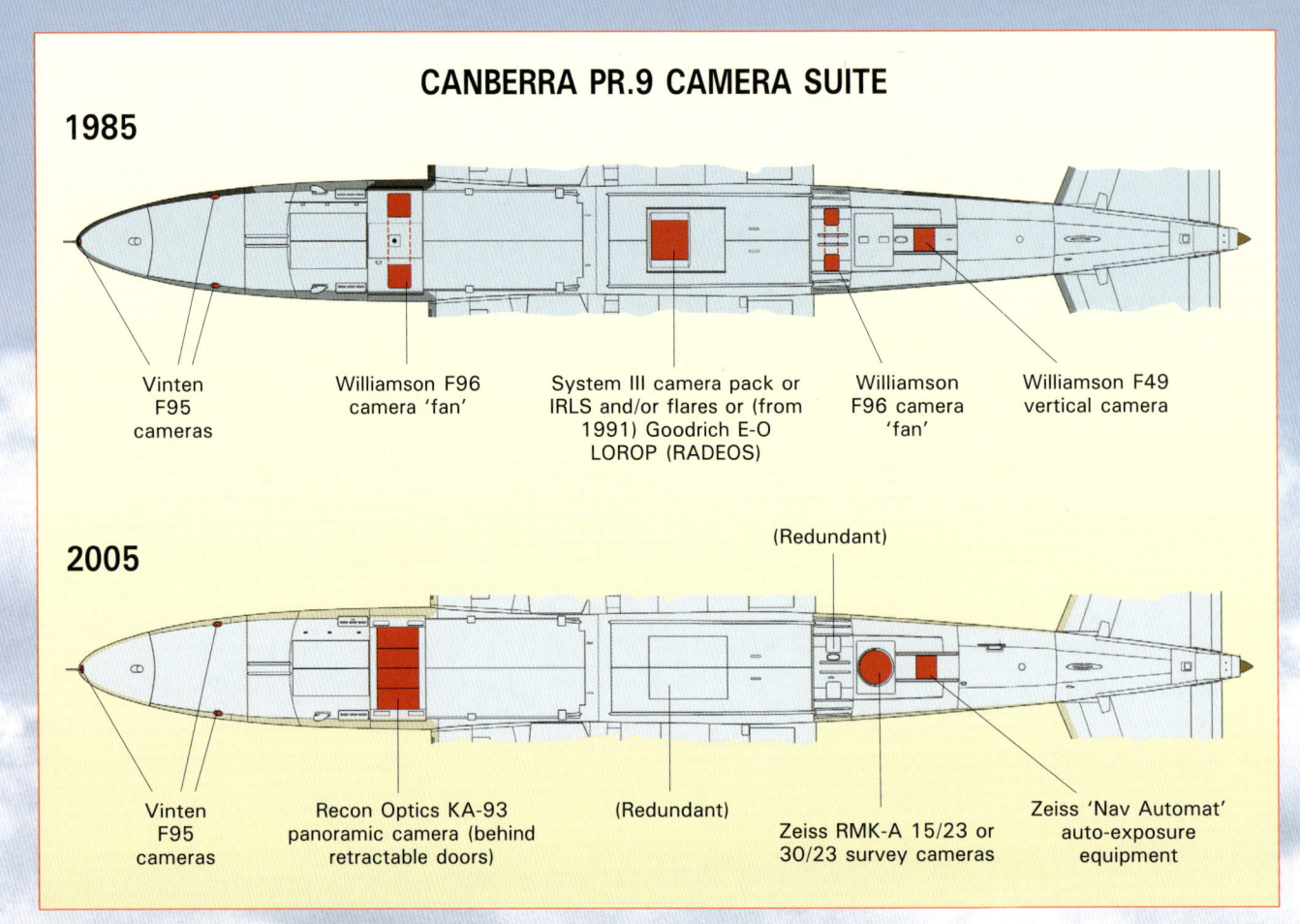

1985

- Vinten F95 cameras
- Williamson F96 camera 'fan'
- System III camera pack or IRLS and/or flares or (from 1991) Goodrich E-O LOROP (RADEOS)
- Williamson F96 camera 'fan'
- Williamson F49 vertical camera

2005

- Vinten F95 cameras
- Recon Optics KA-93 panoramic camera (behind retractable doors)
- (Redundant)
- (Redundant)
- Zeiss RMK-A 15/23 or 30/23 survey cameras
- Zeiss 'Nav Automat' auto-exposure equipment

service much reduced, a major contribution was made during innumerable emergencies, for example the Rwandan refugee crisis (1994–96), the Kosovo 'troubles' (1998–99) and Operation 'Telic', the 2003 Gulf conflict.

Although its airframe was essentially unaltered throughout the PR.9's service life, developments in technology have seen refinements and modifications to its equipment as required by changing threats and working environments. The cameras carried, for example, while always

Above: XH168, in a distinctly bleached-out Hemp paint scheme and carrying the tail insignia of No 1 Photographic Reconnaissance Unit, caught at Wyton on 24 July 1992. Below: XH175 in an earlier image—June 1988—and again sporting No 1 PRU markings.

of extraordinarily high quality, were replaced as their usefulness expired. The Williamson F96 was a standard piece of equipment for much of the aircraft's career, while the three F95s in the nose remained from the time of the its introduction. From the mid 1970s the PR.9s received ARI.18228/6 radar warning receiver (RWR) equipment, housed in a 'cone' at the extreme tail and at the tip of a faired pod mounted on the leading edge of the tailfin, and towards the end of the aircraft's service this was replaced with new RWR systems mounted at each wing tip (the tail 'cones', although redundant, remained *in situ*). Further enhancements included the fitting of a Decca TANS (Tactical Air Navigation System). ARI 5969/3 Infra-Red Line Scan (IRLS) equipment carried by RAF Phantoms was diverted to Wyton when the American jets were retired, and this could be accommodated in the PR.9's bomb bay as an alternative to the standard 36in-focal-length System III 'pointing-lens' camera (as developed for the Lockheed U-2 reconnaissance aircraft). In later years the 36in-focal-length F96 camera 'fan', accommodated forward of the main bay, was deleted in favour of a single 24in-lens Recon Optics KA-93, while the main bay became the location—with difficulty, owing to its dimensions—for RADEOS (Rapid-Deployment Electro-Optical System), manufactured by the Goodrich Corporation and similar to the SYERS (Senior Year Electrooptical Reconnaissance System (also developed for the U-2). Two of these latter systems, one US-owned and the other British-owned, were made available to the PR.9 fleet and were deployed, for example, on a limited basis during 'Telic'.

A MISSING CAPABILITY?

The retirement of the PR.9 has finally removed the 'wet-film' reconnaissance capability from the RAF. Traditional mapping and surveying tasks are henceforth, no doubt, to be undertaken by civilian organisations; military reconnaissance is now, presumably, to be the province of UAVs—and of those, nobody is at the moment saying very much!

MARK NINE 13

DEEP MAINTENANCE

ONE of the reasons for the longevity of the PR.9 was the rigorous servicing and maintenance that attended the aircraft during its career. Practically every aspect of this work — other than pressurisation integrity and major engine refurbishment — was conducted on base by RAF personnel. This spread shows various PR Mk 9 aircraft laid bare, stripped of panelling and access hatches so that the structure of the airframe is revealed for inspection.

Left and below: Maintenance work on Canberra PR.9 XH169 by the Canberra Servicing Flight at RAF Wyton in 1984. The cockpit canopy, navigator's escape hatch, nosewheel assembly and tail cone have been removed, as have the bomb-bay doors. There is of course no hydraulic power, so flaps, forward camera-bay door and wing-mounted air brakes are all relaxed under gravity. Bottom: More recent photographs of the port Avon engine removed (left) and the Avon itself, baffles protecting the delicate structures within. Right: Canberra maintenance by No 39 (1 PRU) Squadron at RAF Marham in the summer of 2005 and (centre right) XH169 in January 2006 being stripped for spares. In the upper photograph, the port-side integral wing fuel tank has been removed and can just be seen ahead of the aircraft.

14 CANBERRA PR9

DEEP MAINTENANCE 15

CHILE CON CANBERRA

THE PR.9 has seen service with one air arm other than the RAF, but the story of its acquisition by the *Fuerza Aérea de Chile* (Chilean Air Force) is beset by rumour—not to say intrigue—for the simple reason that the complete sequence of events leading to that acquisition has never been officially revealed. Facts are hard to come by; hearsay—even today, more than twenty years after the hand-over—flourishes. What is known for certain is as follows.

In the summer of 1982 three RAF Canberra PR Mk 9s had their RAF markings removed, to be replaced with Chilean national *décor*. The aircraft involved were XH166, XH167 and XH173, and these were re-marked, respectively, '341', '342' and '343' though retained the existing disruptive grey/green paint scheme. They were delivered to the *FACh* in October the same year. Aircraft '342' crashed on 24 May 1983 in Chilean Patagonia, both crew members being rescued the next day. The two surviving aircraft have now been withdrawn from service: '341', currently (2006) looking rather the worse for wear, is on display at the Museo Nacional Aeronáutico y del Espacio de Chile (Chilean National Air and Space Museum at the recently closed Los Cerrillos airfield, Santiago; '343' is at the same location, refurbished and resprayed but devoid of national markings.

What is not known is whether these three aircraft were sold to Chile or merely presented; some have suggested that they represented a 'thank you' from the British Government for assistance rendered by Chile during the Falklands War of April–June 1982, sent with a batch of refurbished Hunter jet fighter-bombers. It has been reported, however, that Chilean interest in the PR.9 predated the Falklands conflict by some time, but that the original offer of aircraft was rejected as being too costly. It has also been reported that the loss of one aircraft some months later was the result of a most unusual event: excessive turbulence, it has been claimed, caused the pilot's seat to eject spontaneously.

Other reports suggest that RAF Canberra PR.9s were actually based in Chile for a short while during the Falklands conflict, overflying Argentina and the islands themselves in order to gather intelligence and perhaps even wearing temporary Chilean national markings. It must be stressed that these tales are just that—tales—and have absolutely no official confirmation.

Below PR.9 XH167 at RAF Wyton in September 1982, sporting wing-tip tanks and carrying the Chilean white star on its rudder and the code number '342' on the nosewheel doors.
Bottom: The renovated '343' of the Chilean Air Force (formerly the RAF's XH173) on display at Los Cerrillos, December 2005. The aircraft has been repainted in a close approximation of its original colour scheme but is virtually devoid of markings.

16 CANBERRA PR9

Right and below: Aircraft '341' as she currently appears, incomplete and in very poor condition. The cockpit views at the foot of the page are of '343' prior to the aircraft's restoration.

CHILE CON CANBERRA 17

ON DISPLAY

THROUGHOUT its service, the Canberra was always a favourite with the public, be it on static display at the original Open Days of the 1950s or performing low passes and impressive climb-outs for the huge crowds at the International Air Fairs of more recent years. The summer of 2006 sees the Canberra taking its final bow as a flying participant in Royal Air Force colours, providing spectators with one last opportunity of witnessing its handsome lines and the familiar roar of its two Avon engines.

Below: XH134 about to touch down at RAF Waddington's International Air Show, July 2005.

18 CANBERRA PR9

CANBERRA Mk 9s IN PRESERVATION

The following are known to exist. At the time of writing, it seems likely that at least one of the RAF's final PR Mk 9s will be preserved.

Serial	Location	Remarks
XH132	Italy	SC.9 nose section only. In private ownership.
XH136	Bruntingthorpe, Leics.	Nose section only.
XH165	Blyth Valley, Suffolk	Cockpit section only.
XH166	Los Cerrillos, Chile	Chilean Air Force '341'. Complete airframe.
XH170	RAF Wyton	Gate guardian. Complete airframe.
XH171	RAF Museum Cosford	Complete airframe.
XH173	Los Cerrillos, Chile	Chilean Air Force '343'. Complete airframe.
XH175	Stock, Essex	Nose section only. In private ownership.
XH177	Newark Air Museum, Notts.	Nose section only.

Main image: XH131 executes a low pass at Kleine Brogel, Belgium, July 2005.
Above: The same aircraft at the same show, banking away with air brakes deployed.
Opposite bottom: XH171, on display at RAF Museum Cosford, Shropshire, in the low-level tactical camouflage scheme of the 1980s.
This page, bottom: XH131 making a fast getaway at Fairford, July 2005. The aircraft is only some fifteen feet off the ground but the undercarriage is already practically retracted.

SQUADRONS & COLOURS

WHEN the Canberra PR Mk 9 entered service with the Royal Air Force, it did so as an adjunct to the Service's existing photographic-reconnaissance resources rather than as an entirely novel concept—providing an extension in range, ceiling and capability to squadrons already fulfilling the role. Thus it was in April 1960 that the first half-dozen of the twenty-two PR.9s joined No 58 Squadron at Wyton, Huntingdonshire—which was to remain the PR.9's 'home base' for the next thirty-two years—to be flown along with the Squadron's Canberra PR.7s. These were still the days of 'silver' aircraft, and the colour scheme was sprayed aluminium lacquer overall, relieved by the then-standard Type 'D' roundels (84in diameter for the upper wing surfaces, 36in for the fuselage; it seems unlikely that any PR.9 carried underwing roundels during this era) and appropriate style of fin flashes (24in by 24in square), standard black serial numbers (48in high underwing, 8in high on the rear fuselage) and No 58's perching owl emblem either side of the fin.

By the time the second PR.9 unit, No 13 Squadron, was issued with its new aircraft in the summer of 1961 the type was well established in RAF service. No 13, however, was based at Luqa in Malta, and so began the PR.9's long association with the Mediterranean and Middle-East theatres. As with No 58, No 13's aircraft were sprayed 'silver' with markings as described and the unit emblem—a lynx's head surmounting a dagger—on the fin, the forward upper portion of which latter appeared as a medium grey 'panel'.

The third squadron to be allocated Canberra PR.9s was No 39, also based at Luqa, which took over No 58's aircraft when that unit reverted to being an all-PR.7 operator in November

Right: The first squadron to receive PR.9s was No 58, based at RAF Wyton. This aircraft, XH168, is displaying 244-gallon wing-tip jettison tanks—a common sight on PR Mk 9s in the 1960s and 1970s but rarely if ever carried by this mark in later years. The photograph was taken in September 1962.

Left: A Canberra PR.9 in disruptive camouflage seen over East Anglia, about 1980. The serial number of this aircraft is not known, but the unit emblem of No 39 Squadron can be seen on the fin. Below: XH165, also in disruptive camouflage. The fact that the No 1 PRU emblem is present on the fin suggests that the photograph was taken in the mid-1980s, when all existing RAF PR.9s were allocated to this unit.

1962. These aircraft retained their 'silver' finish, the unit badge being repainted to display No 39's 'winged bomb'. No 58 and No 39 Squadrons continued to range over the Mediterranean, Near East, Middle East and North Africa until late in 1970, when No 39 was recalled to Wyton, leaving No 58 as the principal Canberra reconnaissance unit in those theatres—a duty that it performed for the next six years, whereupon it was disbanded.

The thoroughgoing reassessment of British defence policy that took place in the mid-1960s, with the emphasis switching from high-altitude sorties to low-altitude 'ground-hugging' operations—a logical response to the growing efficacy of anti-aircraft missiles—sounded the death-knell for the postwar 'silver' finish hitherto carried by day combat aircraft as all that might be expected to operate over enemy-held territory were painted in disruptive camouflage (Dark Sea Grey BS 381C-638 and Dark Green BS 381C-641) with under surfaces sprayed Light Aircraft Grey (BS 381C-627). Incongruously, the standard Type 'D' roundels and tri-colour fin flashes were at first retained, but within a short period of time these had been changed to the 'toned-down' red/blue variety; however, unlike other front-line aircraft on the RAF's inventory, the Canberra PR.9s invariably retained a glossy sheen to their paintwork, no doubt because of the need to squeeze the last mile per hour out of the airframes during hazardous reconnaissance sorties.

By the end of 1976 No 13 Squadron, too, had disbanded, leaving No 39 Squadron as the sole Canberra PR.9 operator, but in the summer of 1982 this unit was also due to be disestablished—and so it was, although its aircraft remained *in situ*, equipping the newly reformed No 1 Photographic Reconnaissance Unit. Many of No 39 Squadron's personnel remained with the aircraft, while the only obvious change to the latter's paintwork was the renewal of the insignia on the fin.

SQUADRONS & COLOURS 21

In the meantime, however, another major revision to the airframe's paintwork was taking place as the Dark Sea Grey and Dark Green disruptive camouflage gave way to Hemp (BS 4800:10-B-21)—reputedly to match the concrete on which parked aircraft were from time to time dispersed. The Light Aircraft Grey undersurfaces were retained, and the entire finish was semi-gloss ('satin') in character; Victor and VC-10 aerial tankers were similarly modified. This scheme, introduced from the mid-1980s, was retained for home-based PR.9s until the aircraft finally left service, although the method of displaying the national markings changed significantly over those years.

Above (clockwise from top left): The No 1 PRU emblem on XH136; No 1 PRU's emblem on a Hemp-finished XH134; a new rendition of the No 13 Squadron badge on XH136 seen in October 1991; and the No 39 (1 PRU) Squadron insignia in 2005.

22 CANBERRA PR9

Above: A portrait of XH135 in 1991 with No 13 Squadron markings, celebrating fifty years of Canberra operations for the RAF.
Below: XH170, the gate guardian at RAF Wyton—home to Canberra squadrons for forty years from 1953 until 1993.

To begin with, the red/blue 84in and 36in roundels were retained, although the fin flash was reduced in width to 18in, but the entire ensemble stood out starkly against the Hemp paintwork and rather defeated the object of the 'low-visibility' overall finish. A decade later, however, the dark shades of the national insignia had been reduced to pink and pale blue, making them barely noticeable. Fuselage serials were usually still 8in in height, generally in black at first but with the introduction of the pink/blue roundels beginning to appear in white; the fin flashes were reduced in size to 1ft square. Underwing serials vanished altogether with the old Dark Sea Grey/Dark Green camouflage, never to be seen again. During the final years of service the roundels were reduced in size to 18in in diameter in all six positions.

During this period No 39 Squadron was re-established and the PR.9 unit became known officially as No 39 (1 PRU) Squadron. Again the aircraft changed little in terms of their markings, the only distinguishing characteristic being the reintroduction of the 'winged bomb' in place of 1 PRU's 'globe' insignia—though not all the aircraft were redecorated immediately. A white two-letter code starting with 'A' was generally to be seen at the base of the fin.

ROYAL AIR FORCE CANBERRA PR Mk 9 UNITS AND SQUADRONS

Unit	Base	Dates	Remarks
No 58 Squadron	Wyton	Apr 1960–Nov 1962	
No 13 Squadron	Akrotiri (Cyprus)	Jul 1961–1 Sep 1965	Mediterranean-based for entire period. Disbanded as a result of run-down of Near East Air Force.
	Luqa (Malta)	1 Sep 1965–6 Jan 1972	
	Akrotiri	6 Jan–10 Oct 1972	
	Luqa	10 Oct 1972–Oct 1976	
No 39 Squadron	Luqa	Nov 1962–Oct 1970	Inherited aircraft from No 58 Squadron.
	Wyton	Oct 1970–2 Jun 1982	Mainly tactical reconnaissance from 1972.
	Wyton	Jul 1992–Dec 1993	Officially titled No 39 (1 PRU) Squadron from July 1992.
	Marham	Dec 1993–31 Jul 2006	Final PR.9 operations.
No 1 Photographic Reconnaissance Unit	Wyton	2 Jun 1982–Jul 1992	Aircraft transferred from No 39 Squadron.

SQUADRONS & COLOURS 23

One final change to the Canberra's external finish took place during the last years of operations. In the 1990s the Ministry of Defence decreed that certain aircraft operating out-of-area on deployment should receive an application of Alkali Removable Temporary Finish, and thus Canberra PR.9s deploying to, for example, Oman, were sprayed overall ARTF light grey. Matt in character, this coating quickly succumbed to weathering and general wear and tear, revealing the underlying Hemp around such areas as the cockpit, wing leading edges and walkways; further, oil stains bled freely through the finish at joints and panel junctions, noticeably discolouring

Above: Embellishments (clockwise from top left)— XH131 in 1998, with 'winged bomb' and Squadron Leader's rank flag; 'Scud'-hunting symbols on XH135, 2003; nose art on XH168, 2003; and nose art on XH169, again in 2003.

24 CANBERRA PR9

SQUADRONS & COLOURS 25

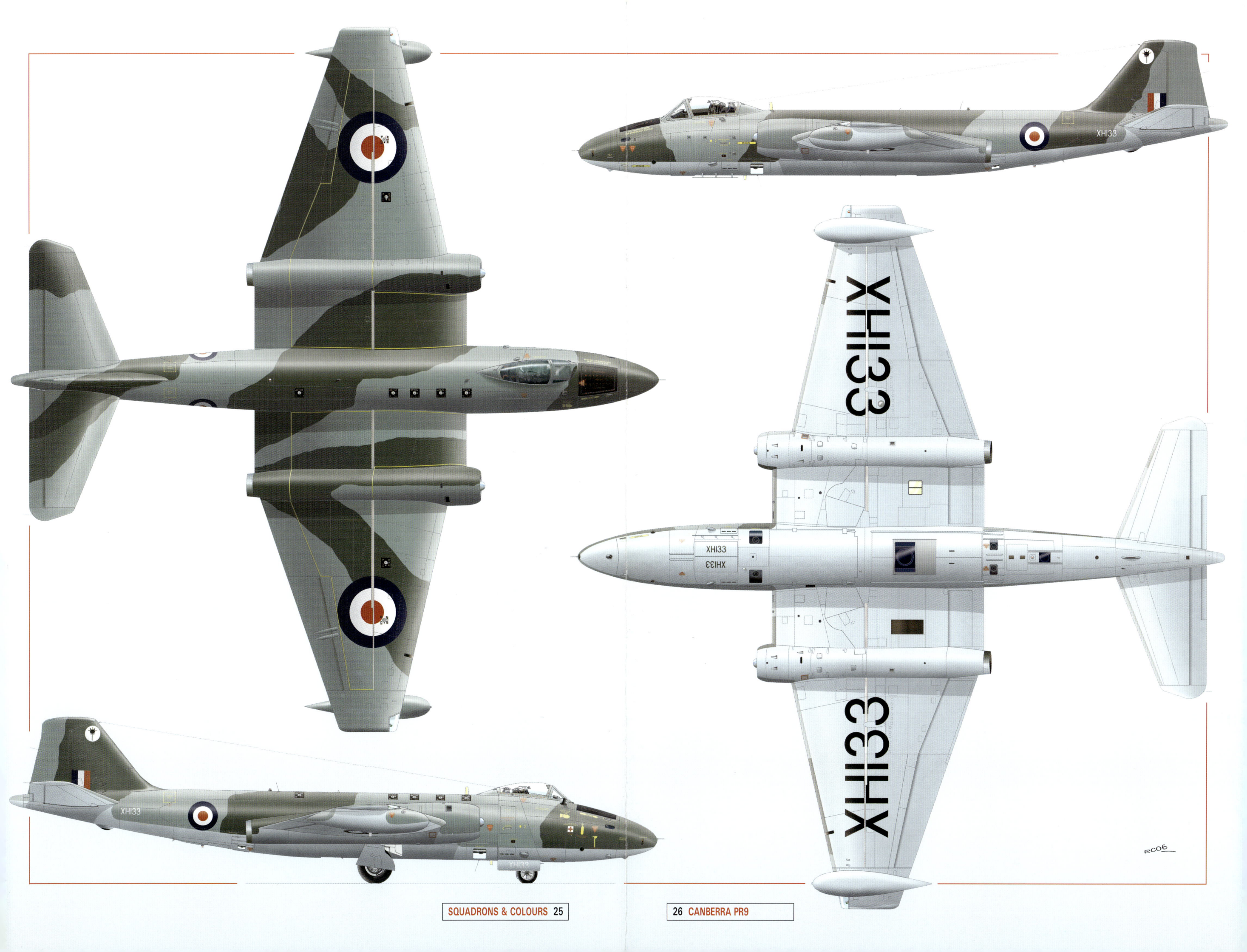

26 CANBERRA PR9

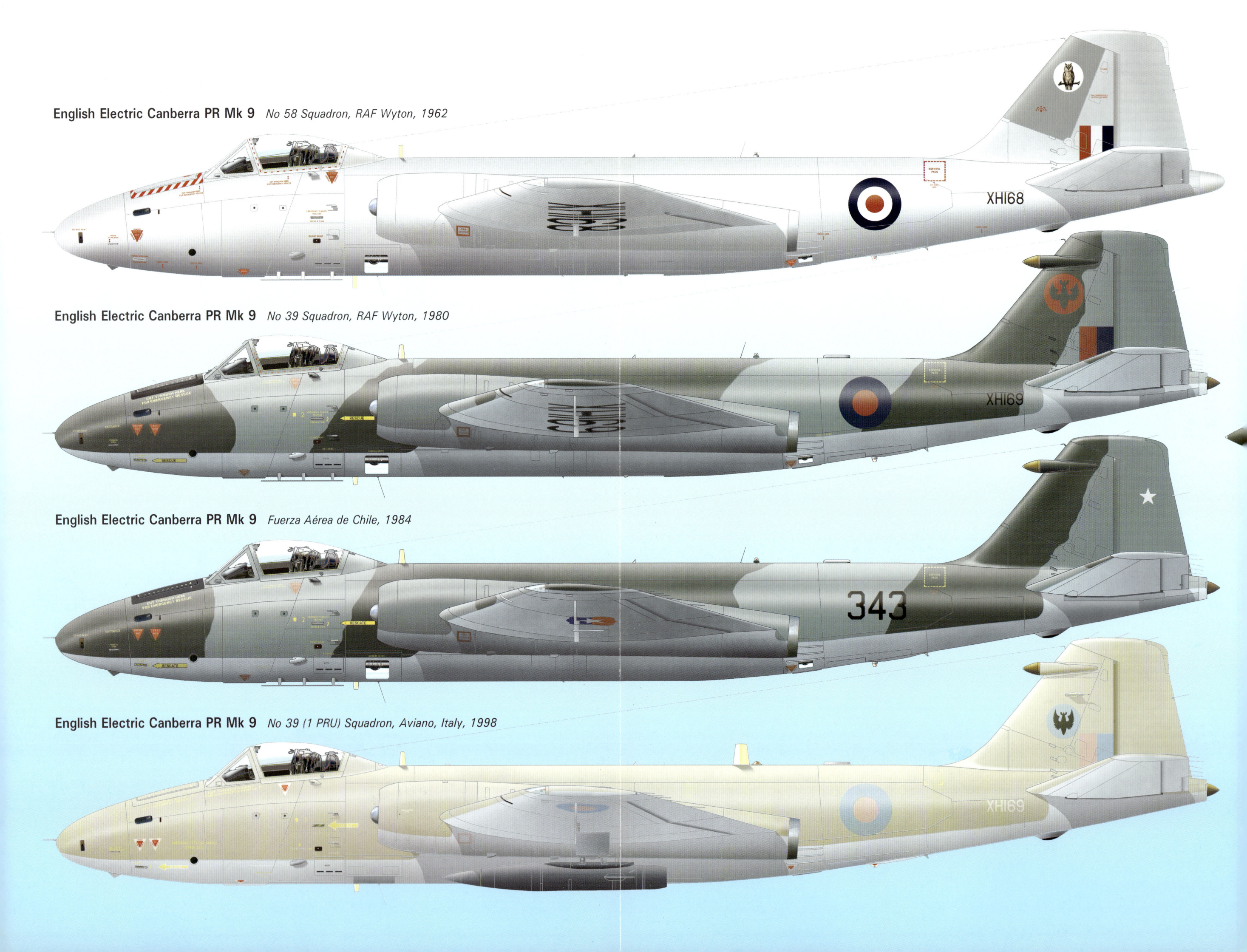

English Electric Canberra PR Mk 9 *No 58 Squadron, RAF Wyton, 1962*

English Electric Canberra PR Mk 9 *No 39 Squadron, RAF Wyton, 1980*

English Electric Canberra PR Mk 9 *Fuerza Aérea de Chile, 1984*

English Electric Canberra PR Mk 9 *No 39 (1 PRU) Squadron, Aviano, Italy, 1998*

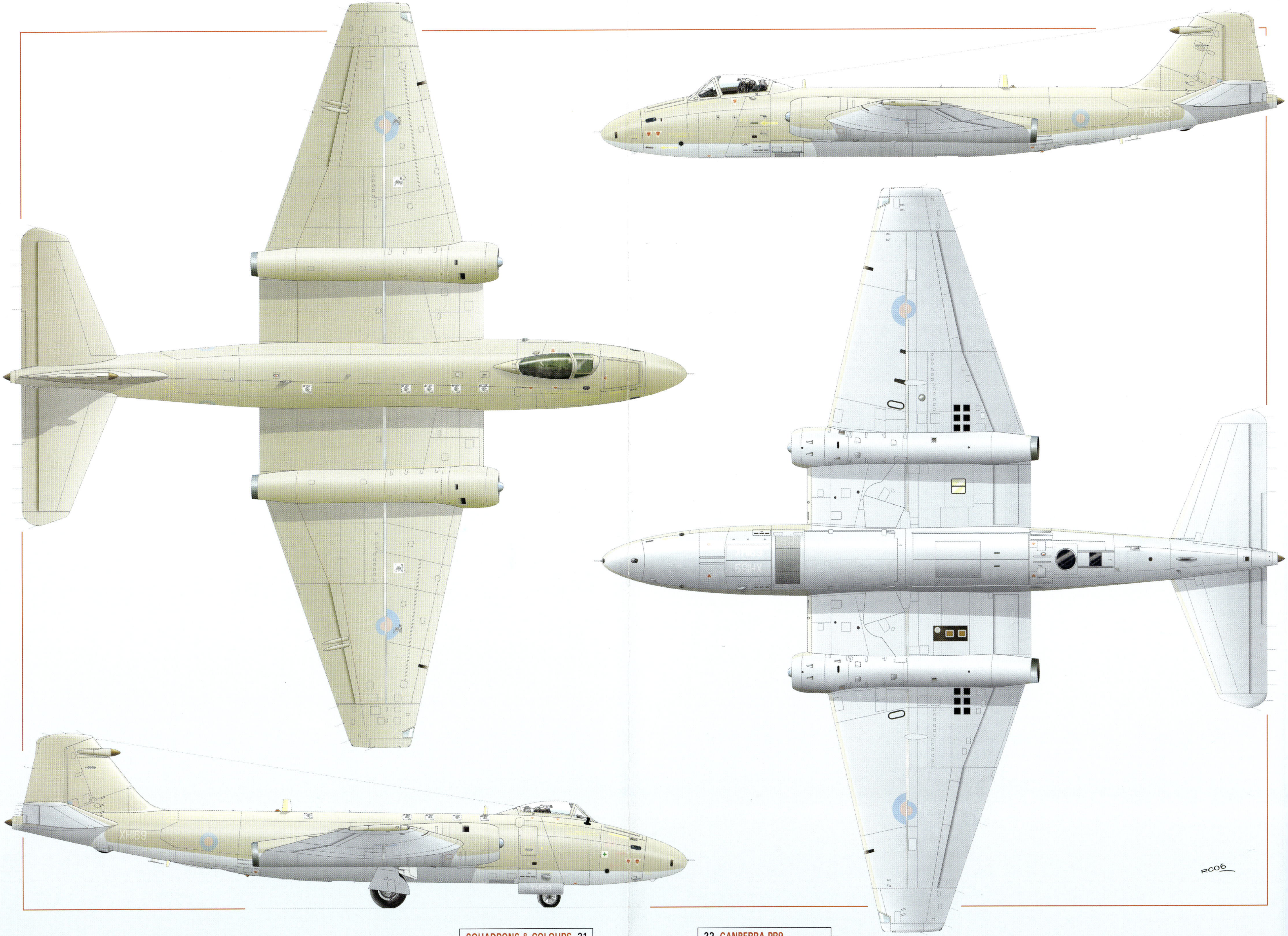

SQUADRONS & COLOURS 31 | 32 CANBERRA PR9

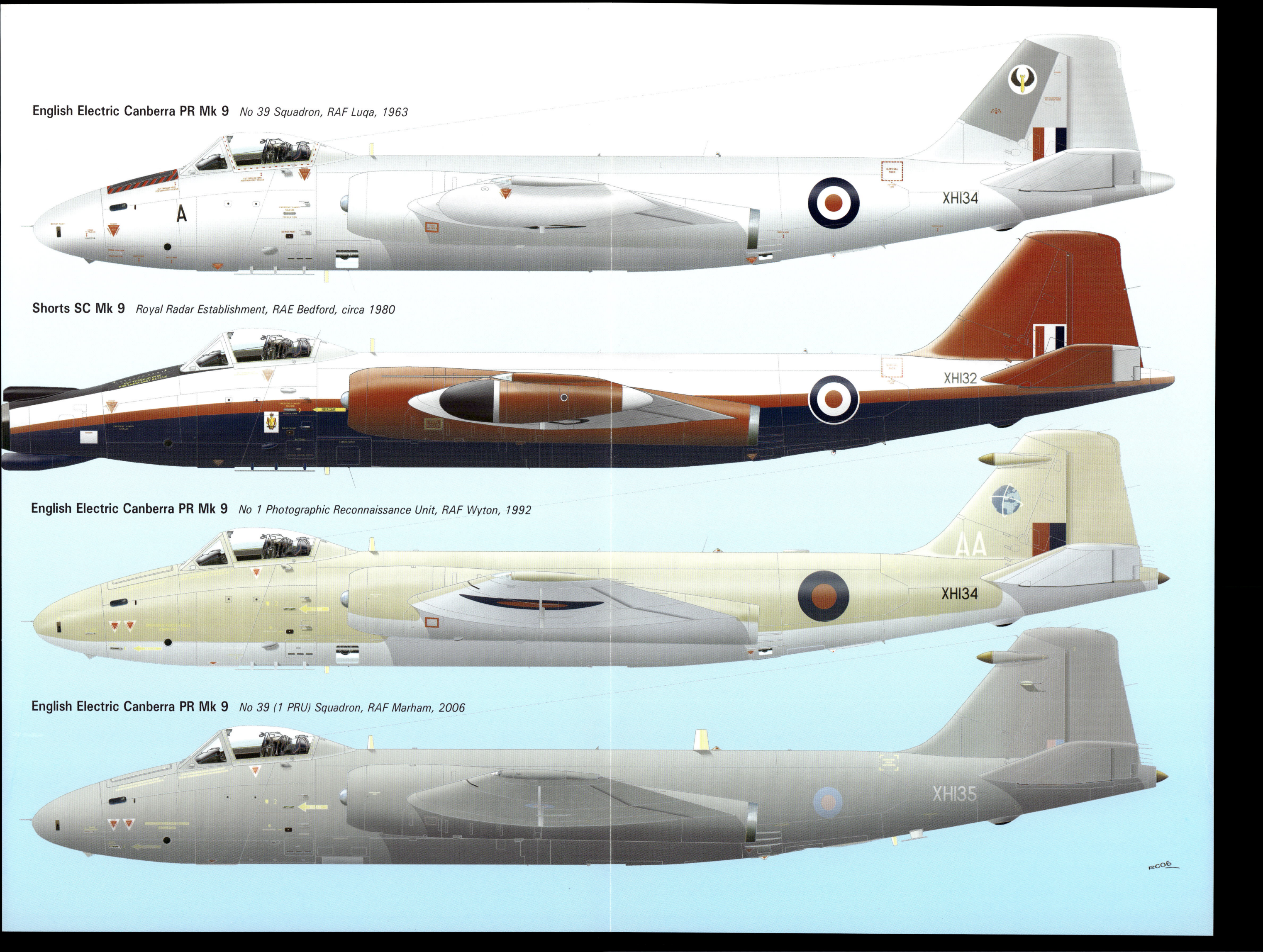

English Electric Canberra PR Mk 9 *No 39 Squadron, RAF Luqa, 1963*

Shorts SC Mk 9 *Royal Radar Establishment, RAE Bedford, circa 1980*

English Electric Canberra PR Mk 9 *No 1 Photographic Reconnaissance Unit, RAF Wyton, 1992*

English Electric Canberra PR Mk 9 *No 39 (1 PRU) Squadron, RAF Marham, 2006*

Above: When No 39 (1PRU) Squadron deployed to Oman in 2005 the aircraft carried an overall coating of ARTF, as seen here in this image of XH169 being manoeuvred back into her hangar.
Right: XH135 on the same deployment. The gradual erosion of the ARTF is becoming evident.
Below: The PR.9 was the only mark of Canberra to feature an upward-hinging canopy, but although this provided plenty of ventilation when the aircraft was on the ground a temporary heat shield over the glazing was still necessary in the baking sun of the Middle East. This is XH169 again.

the paintwork. The application required all minor airframe notices and markings to be carefully masked off, and hence the original Hemp was detectable between individual characters and numerals (as a close examination of the relevant photographs in this book will show), although unit insignia were painted over. The ARTF could, with some effort, be scrubbed off with a water-based solution when no longer required.

SQUADRONS & COLOURS 33

ENTRANCE OTHER SIDE

ALL military aircraft carry official warning notices, advisory information for servicing crews and standard symbols (usually) denoting various materials and substances—frequently hazardous—that are contained in the workings, but the Canberra PR.9 went rather further than most in its display of adornments. Refuelling points were prominently marked on fuselage and upper wing surfaces, notices and symbols relating to rescue procedures and the location of rescue equipment virtually covered the nose area, and the walkway boundaries for maintenance personnel were marked off in the usual way. However, over forty-plus years the style of these markings has changed, as these images show…

Main image: The hard-worked XH169, undergoing maintenance in the summer of 2005. Eagle-eyed Canberra enthusiasts will notice something odd about one of the equipment notices!

34 CANBERRA PR9

Above: ARTF overall—except inside the lettering—early 2006.

Opposite page: The relative simplicity of the early-style PR.9 symbology: everything in red or black—and no rescue arrows.
Below: Neat presentation of crew names on XH165, June 1984.

ENTRANCE OTHER SIDE 35

IN DETAIL

Left: Forward fuselage details (XH134), January 2006, showing the F95 camera port in the extreme nose, with the pitot sensor immediately above; the tagged static pressure inlet (feeding the aircraft's altimeter systems); the navigator's direct-vision window—one each side, the navigator's only contact with the outside world, and known colloquially as the 'day/night indicator'(!); and, further aft, the starboard F95 camera port.

Main image: Nose details, XH134—the same aircraft in an earlier (July 2005) finish—showing the crew entry facilities. The specially designed PR.9 pilot's access steps clamped neatly into recesses in the fuselage skin; the navigator's position forward was afforded access by activating the release handle clearly seen. The triangular fairing beneath the hinged nose section was the navigator's 'recce viewfinder', enabling him to see beneath the aircraft in an arc from forward to aft.

38 CANBERRA PR9

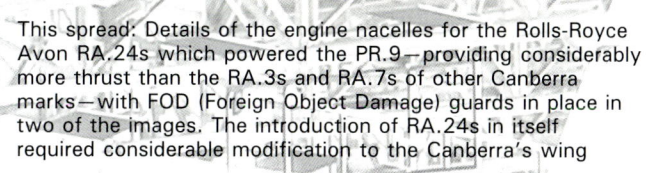

This spread: Details of the engine nacelles for the Rolls-Royce Avon RA.24s which powered the PR.9 – providing considerably more thrust than the RA.3s and RA.7s of other Canberra marks – with FOD (Foreign Object Damage) guards in place in two of the images. The introduction of RA.24s in itself required considerable modification to the Canberra's wing design owing to their greater dimensions. Typically for a parked aircraft, the split flaps are drooped, the bomb-bay doors are open and the doors for the forward equipment bay (starboard side) and battery access (port) are lowered. In the photograph lower left, the Mk 7B radio altimeter panel can just be made out on the wing surface inboard of the Avon nacelle.

IN DETAIL 39

40 CANBERRA PR9

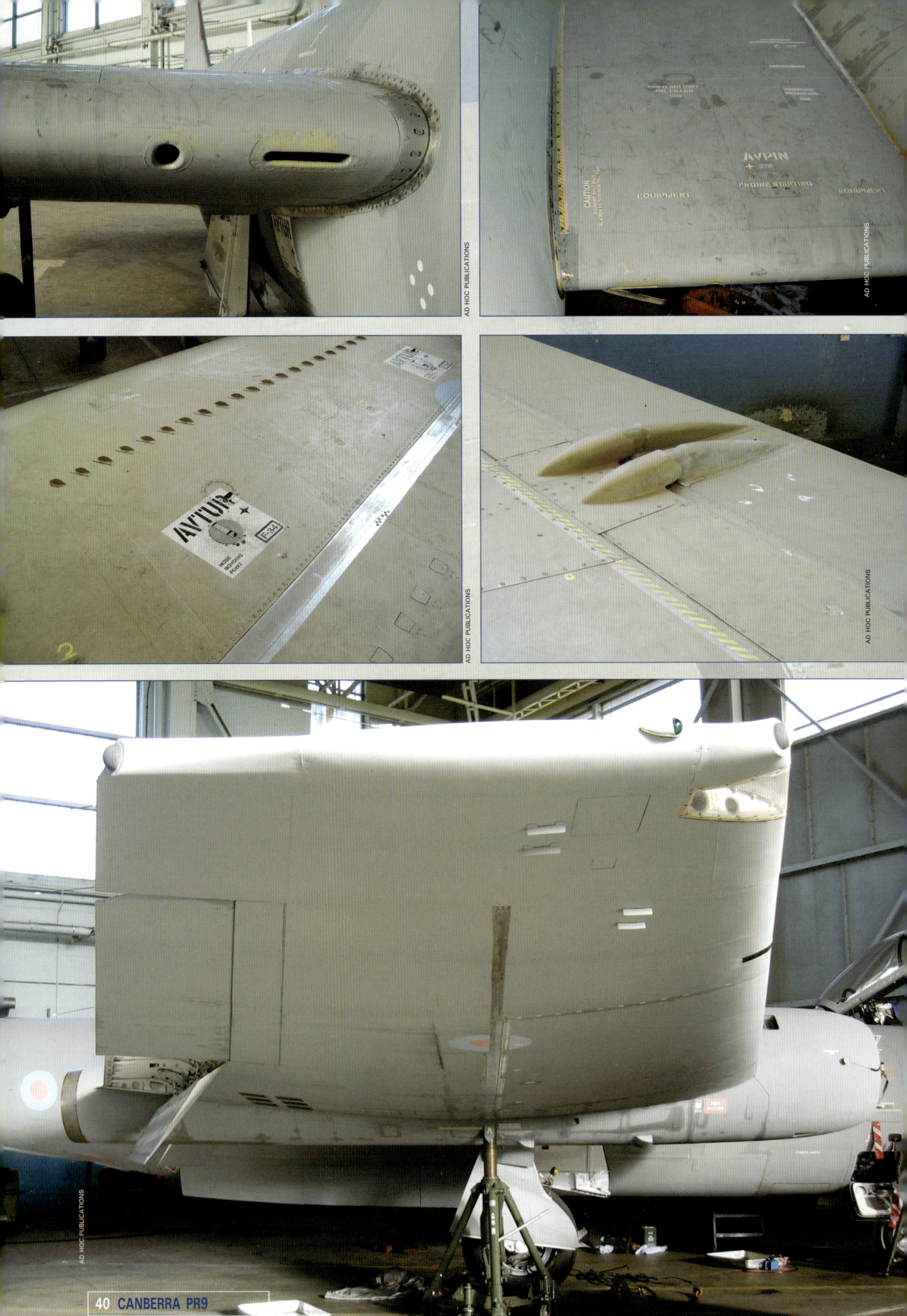

Opposite page: With an area of over 1,000 square feet, the PR.9's wing was of impressive dimensions for an aircraft of this size. The outboard sections forward of the main spar were integral fuel tanks and were removable as complete units (and of course interchangeable with those of other PR.9s—which explains the mismatched roundel 'halves' frequently noted on the wings). The position of the main spar is clearly shown: the panelling along its length, above and below, was usually left unpainted to facilitate fatigue inspection. Also shown in close-up here are the characteristic vortex generators, and the actuator fairings for the control surfaces. The colours of the walkway markings on Hemp-finished aircraft were often to be seen reversed.

This page: Inboard lower wing and nacelle surfaces (above left and below), with oil streaking very evident on the latter. The renewal of the RWR (radar warning receiver) equipment necessitated modifications to the wing tip and wing-tip lights (above). The under surfaces of the wing featured further vortex generators towards the tip; these 'aerodynamic crutches' were present also low on the tailfin.

IN DETAIL 41

This page and opposite, bottom: Rear fuselage details. Uniquely in the RAF in the twenty-first century, the PR.9 required the services of a carpenter from time to time since a proportion of the vertical tail was fabricated from birch and plywood. These photographs also show the tail bumper and fuel vent; the location of the survival pack ahead of the fin; the dorsal combined VHF/UHF antenna for the No 2 radio system, the anti-collision light and (half-way between the blade antenna and the tailfin) the antenna for the Embedded GPS/Inertial (EGI) navigation system (replacing the earlier, larger, oval fairing); and the lower UHF aerial. The paired strips beneath the fuselage (repeated at other locations along the belly) activated the fire suppression systems in the event of the aircraft making a wheels-up landing. Opposite page, upper: Features at the tail redundant during the final years: the ILS (Instrument Landing System) localiser aerials, replaced by sensors along the wing leading edges; and the ARI.18228 Sky Guardian RWR, replaced by new RWR at the wing tips (although the old 'cones' remained in place to the end).

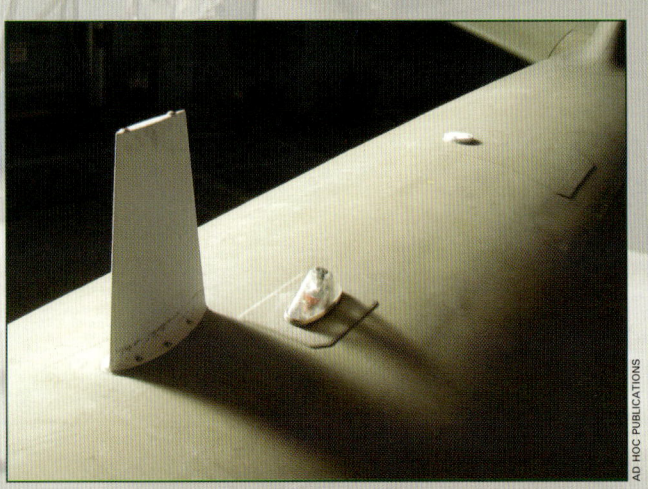

42 CANBERRA PR9

IN DETAIL 43

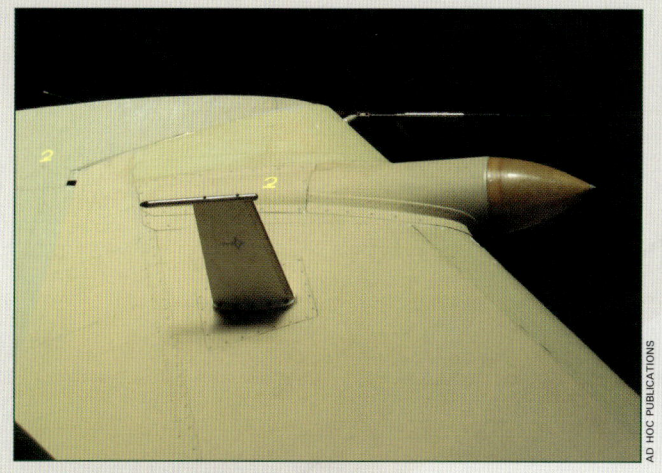

CANBERRA PR9

This spread: Under the tail, Marham, 2005. The tailplane, with a degree of dihedral, featured elevators and trim tabs and was also of limited variable incidence (the associated gap at the tailplane root is apparent here). The trailing edges of all the flying surfaces were liberally equipped with static dischargers. In keeping with general RAF practice, the upper-surface colour 'wrapped' the wing and tailplane leading edges. The offset ventral anti-collision light seen immediately aft of the bomb bay occupied various positions throughout the PR.9's career as upgrades and changes of photographic equipment demanded that it be relocated. Shown in the photograph below are the 'honeycomb' effect across the surface of the former RWR tail cone and the after navigation light just beneath the base of the rudder.

IN DETAIL 45

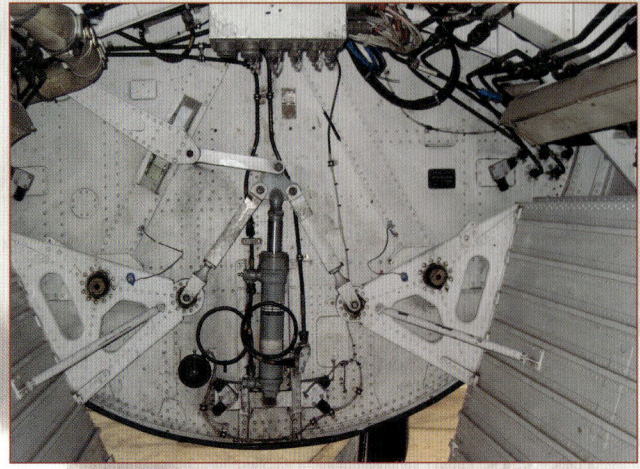

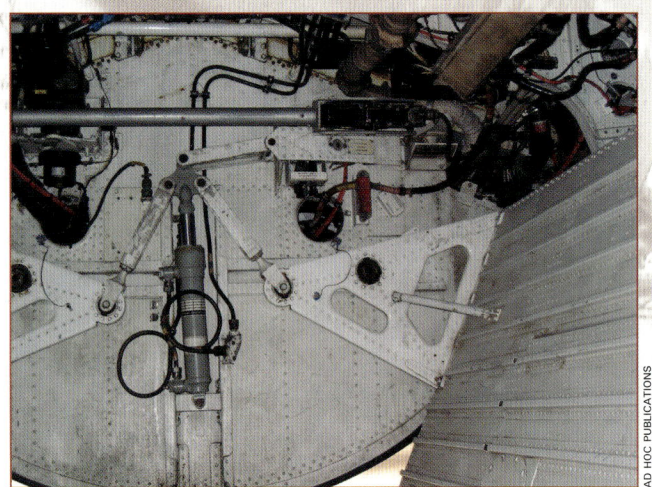

This spread: Details of the bomb bay intact (above and top right: looking forward; above right: looking aft) and with doors removed (immediately right). In latter years the main bay (or flare bay), hitherto housing the System III camera pack, was from time to time the location for the Goodrich electro-optical (E-O) LOROP (Long-Range Oblique Photography) survey sensor—known also in the RAF as the RADEOS (Rapid-Deployment Electro-Optical System). Twenty years separate the two images below: on the left, the RMK-A hatch is swung down (2005); on the right, the same compartment houses the earlier type of radio altimeter equipment. The bay immediately forward of this one was home to one of two 'fan of two' F96 systems carried by the PR.9 for much of its career but by 2005, as can be seen, this compartment was redundant and 'windowless'. The photograph opposite shows the rearmost camera hatch—that seen also below left— open to reveal a Zeiss RMK-A 15/23, immediately in front of which are (left to right) the ventral anti-collision light, crash strips and TACAN antenna.

46 CANBERRA PR9

IN DETAIL 47

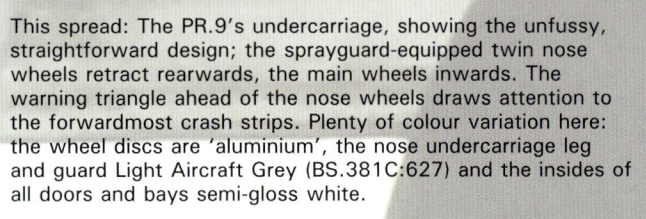

This spread: The PR.9's undercarriage, showing the unfussy, straightforward design; the sprayguard-equipped twin nose wheels retract rearwards, the main wheels inwards. The warning triangle ahead of the nose wheels draws attention to the forwardmost crash strips. Plenty of colour variation here: the wheel discs are 'aluminium', the nose undercarriage leg and guard Light Aircraft Grey (BS.381C:627) and the insides of all doors and bays semi-gloss white.

48 CANBERRA PR9

IN DETAIL 49

INSIDE INFO

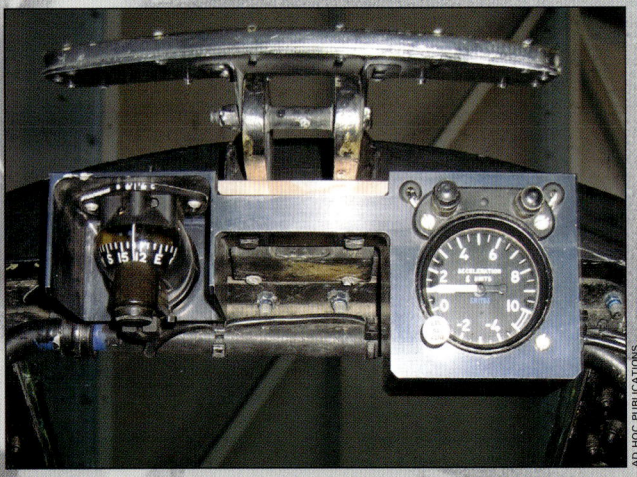

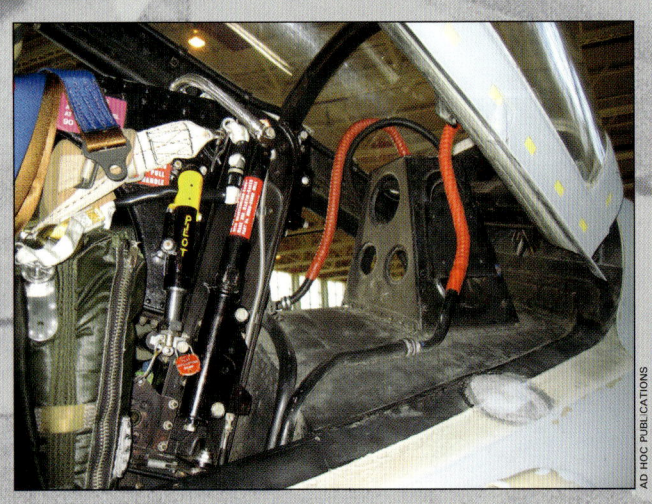

50 CANBERRA PR9

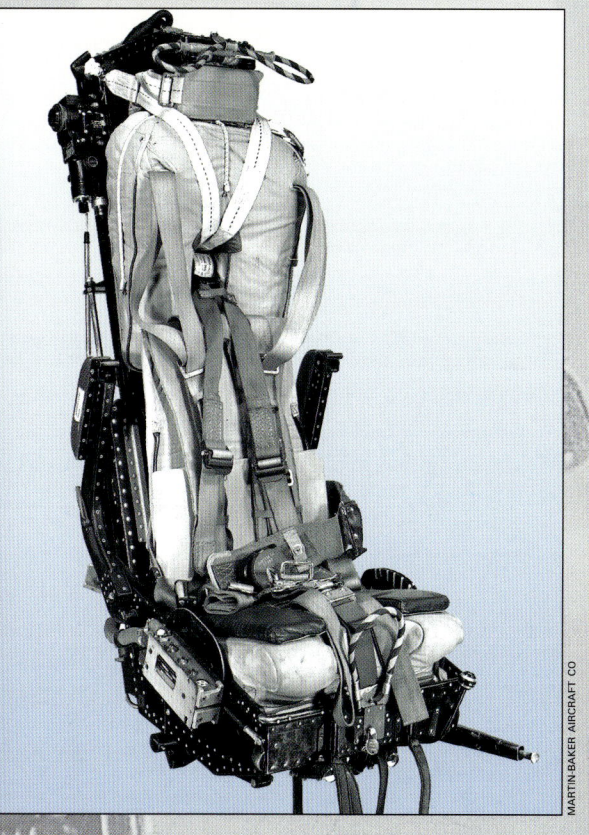

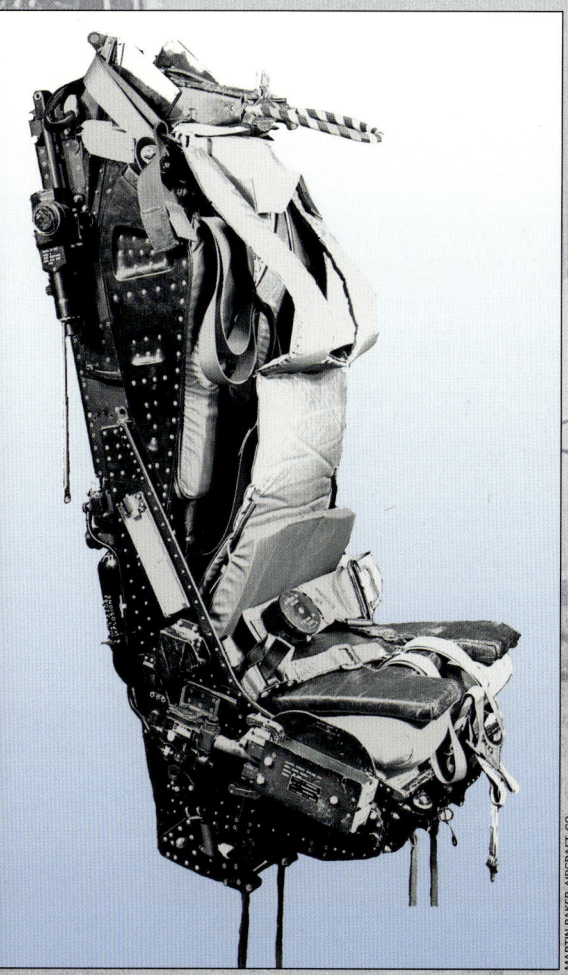

Opposite page: Close up within the cockpit, showing the range of traditional instruments and with scant evidence of upgrades since the aircraft's introduction to service. Centre left: The pilot's and navigator's seats differed, that for the pilot (upper photograph) being designated Type 3CS and that for the navigator (lower) Type 4QS. Above and immediately left: The interior of the navigator's compartment (above: with folding chart table prominent). During PR.9 servicing, if the Avon engines were removed the floor of the navigator's position would be piled high with weighting (left, lower) in order to help keep the aircraft in a stable and horizontal attitude — 'trestle heres' notwithstanding

INSIDE INFO 51

SCALE PLANS

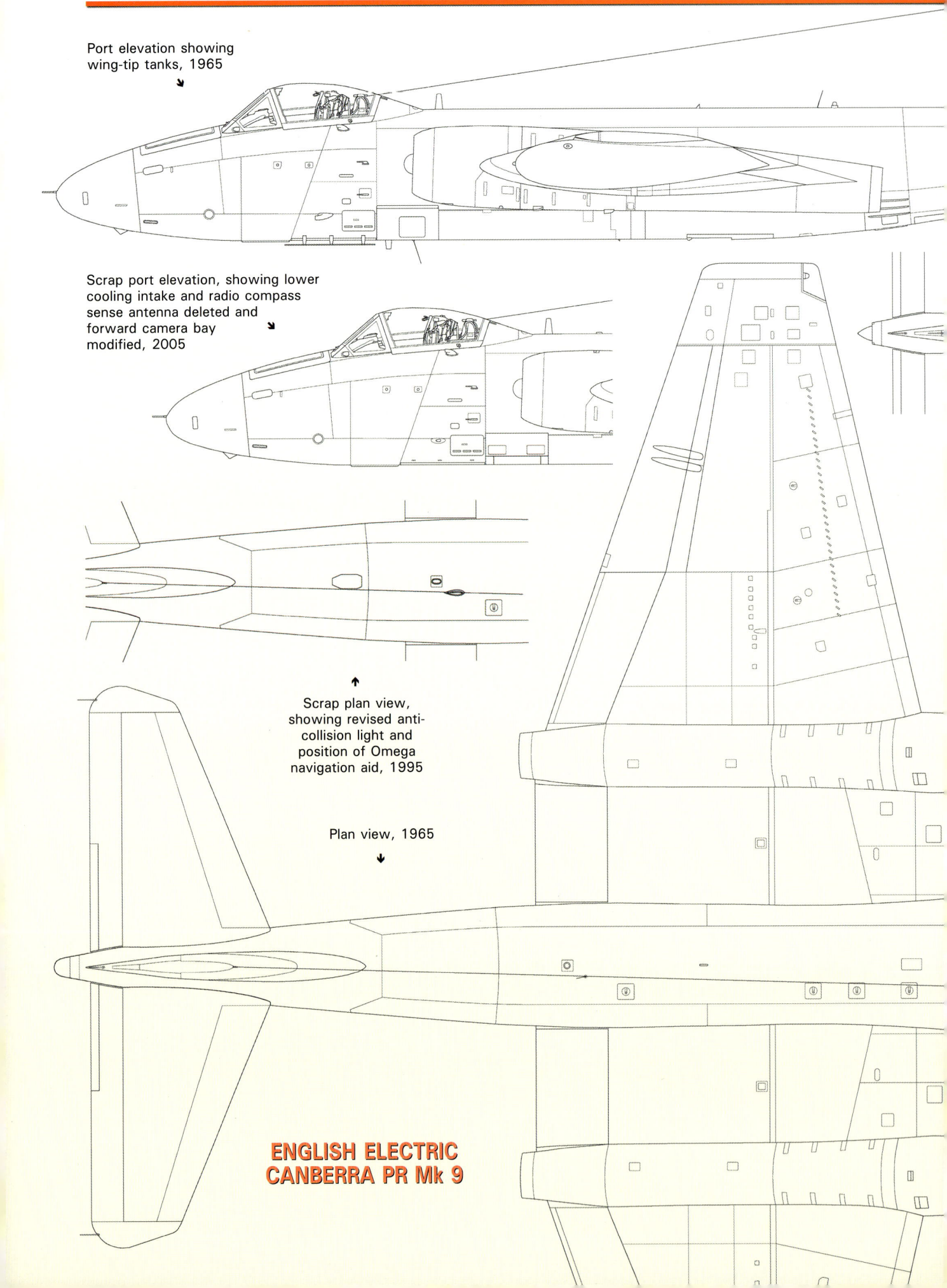

Port elevation showing wing-tip tanks, 1965

Scrap port elevation, showing lower cooling intake and radio compass sense antenna deleted and forward camera bay modified, 2005

Scrap plan view, showing revised anti-collision light and position of Omega navigation aid, 1995

Plan view, 1965

ENGLISH ELECTRIC CANBERRA PR Mk 9

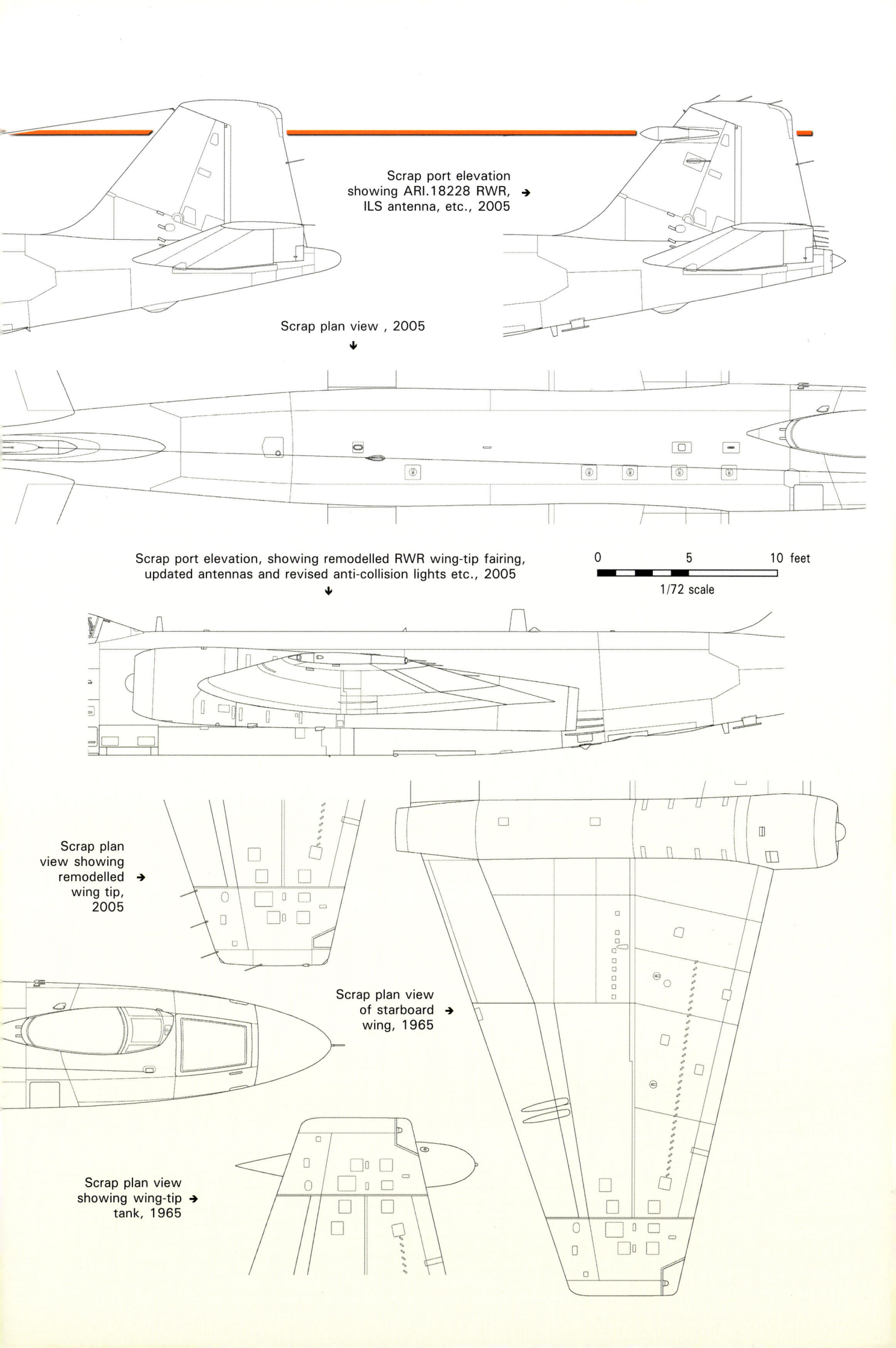

Scrap port elevation showing ARI.18228 RWR, ILS antenna, etc., 2005 →

Scrap plan view, 2005 ↓

Scrap port elevation, showing remodelled RWR wing-tip fairing, updated antennas and revised anti-collision lights etc., 2005 ↓

0   5   10 feet
1/72 scale

Scrap plan view showing remodelled wing tip, 2005 →

Scrap plan view of starboard wing, 1965 →

Scrap plan view showing wing-tip tank, 1965 →

0   5   10 feet
1/72 scale

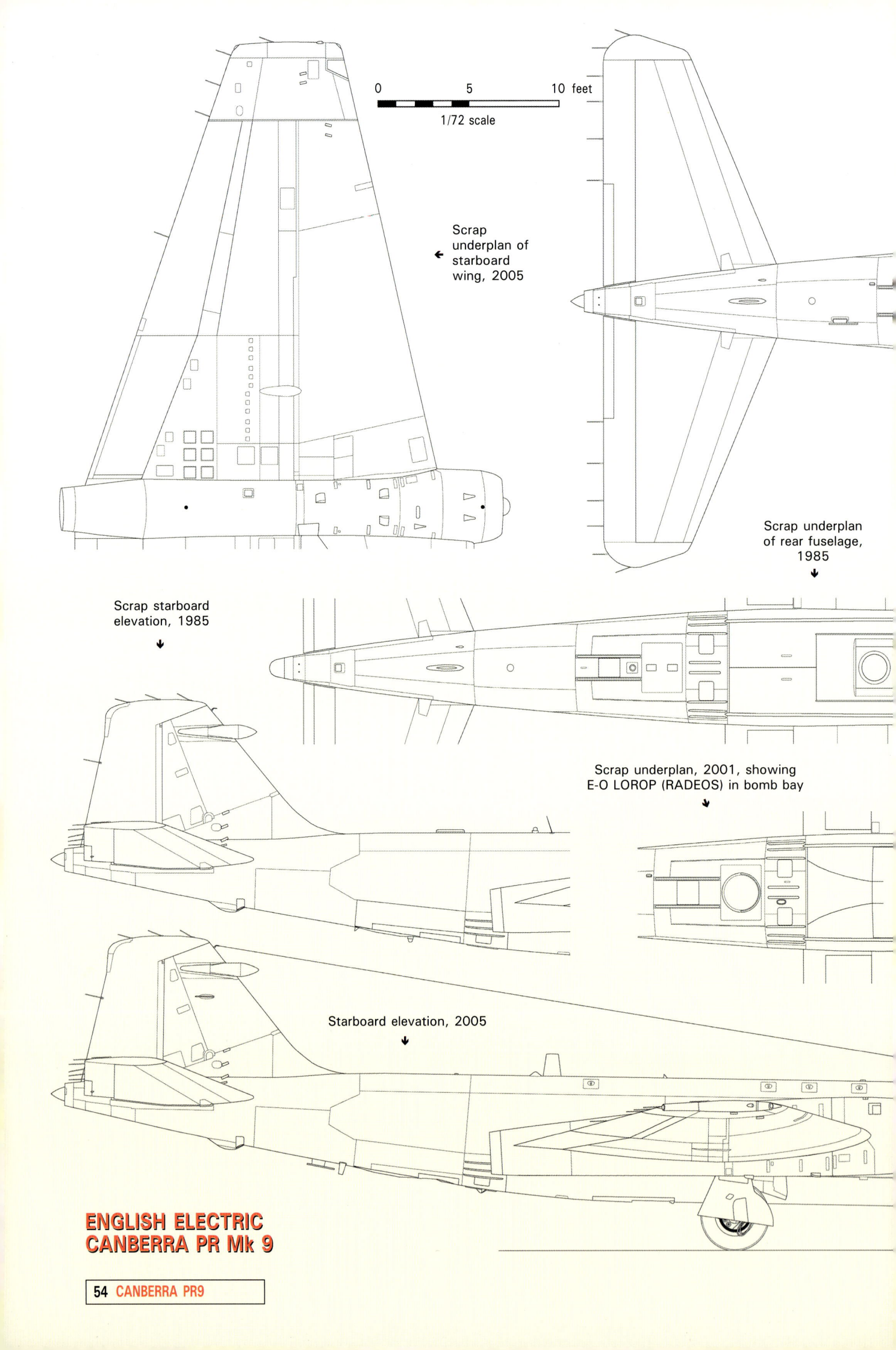

Scrap underplan of starboard wing, 2005 ←

Scrap underplan of rear fuselage, 1985 ↓

Scrap starboard elevation, 1985 ↓

Scrap underplan, 2001, showing E-O LOROP (RADEOS) in bomb bay ↓

Starboard elevation, 2005 ↓

ENGLISH ELECTRIC CANBERRA PR Mk 9

54 CANBERRA PR9

Scrap underplan of wing tip, 1965

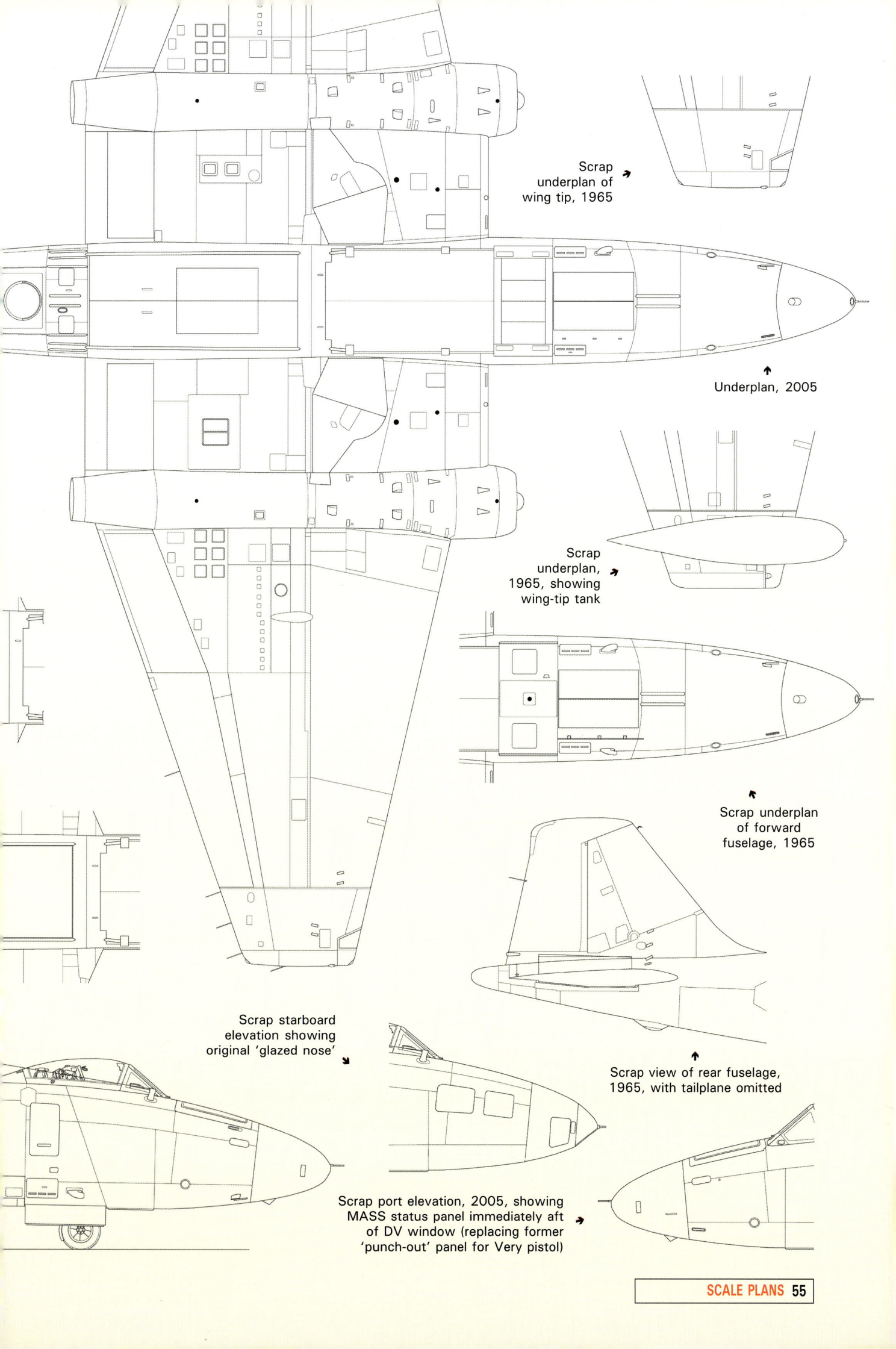

Underplan, 2005

Scrap underplan, 1965, showing wing-tip tank

Scrap underplan of forward fuselage, 1965

Scrap starboard elevation showing original 'glazed nose'

Scrap view of rear fuselage, 1965, with tailplane omitted

Scrap port elevation, 2005, showing MASS status panel immediately aft of DV window (replacing former 'punch-out' panel for Very pistol)

SCALE PLANS 55

SHORTS SC.9

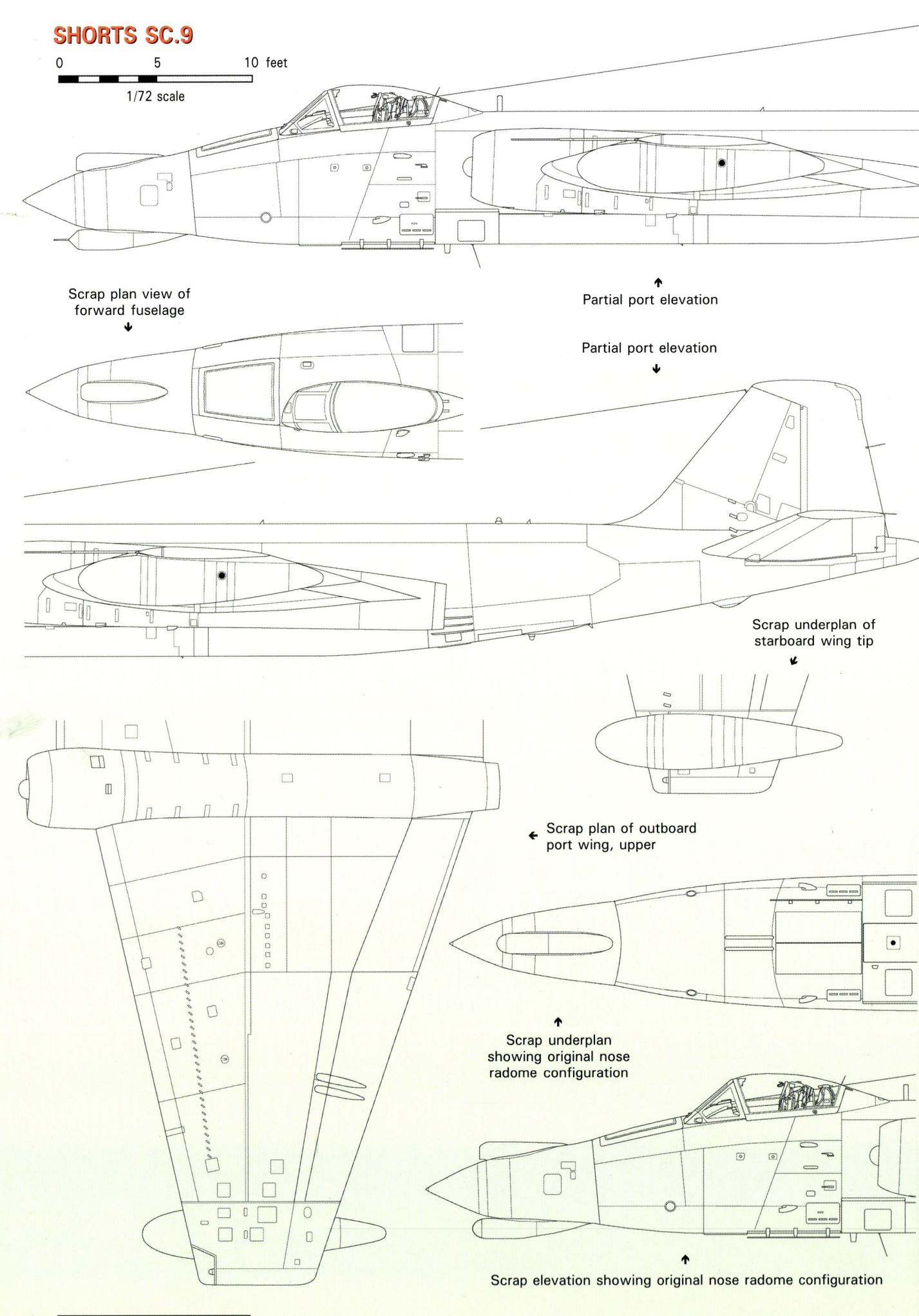

0 5 10 feet
1/72 scale

Scrap plan view of forward fuselage ↓

Partial port elevation ↑

Partial port elevation ↓

Scrap underplan of starboard wing tip ↓

← Scrap plan of outboard port wing, upper

Scrap underplan showing original nose radome configuration ↑

Scrap elevation showing original nose radome configuration ↑

56 CANBERRA PR9